LONDON UNDERGROUND
Ghost Stories

Prepare to be frightened by these terrifying tales and
mysterious events from the London Underground

By

Jill Armitage

BRADWELL
BOOKS

Published by Bradwell Books
9 Orgreave Close Sheffield S13 9NP

Email: books@bradwellbooks.co.uk
© Jill Armitage 2014

All rights reserved. No part of this publication may be
produced, stored in a retrieval system or transmitted in any
form or by any means, electronic, mechanical, photocopying,
recording or otherwise without the prior permission of
Bradwell Books.

British Library Cataloguing in Publication Data: a catalogue
record for this book is available from the British Library.
1st Edition

ISBN: 9781902674711

Design by: jenksdesign@yahoo.co.uk
Print: Gomer Press, Llandysul, Ceredigion SA44 4JL

Photography Credits: unless indicated all images Jill Armitage
& front cover Shutterstock/Luciano Mortula. Photograph on
page 51 The Society for Psychical Research
Illustrations by Jill Armitage and Lauren Richards

The Underground logo is ® Transport for London

CONTENTS

INTRODUCTION

Great Britain has led the world in nearly every aspect of railway development, and the London Metropolitan Railway, the first underground railway in the world, celebrated one hundred and fifty years of transport service to London in 2013.

Initially it was not a proper underground railway; it was a covered way, more like a shallow trench which didn't go to any great depth. The steam locomotives were noisy, sooty and smoky, filling the tunnels and passages with poisonous and almost impenetrable steam and smoke. Openings were made in the roof

A busy scene on the London Underground
(bronze by Paul Day at St Pancras Station)

to provide a small amount of ventilation and daylight, while artificial illumination was provided by gas lighting from suspended glass globes. Even the wooden carriages had the novel introduction of gas light. This original mode of transport was viewed with wonder and trepidation, and when the four-mile stretch of the London Metropolitan Railway between Farringdon and Paddington opened on 10 January 1863, it carried 38,000 passengers.

In 1868, the District Railway was opened, running between South Kensington and Westminster. The 'Met' and the 'District' were so popular that they were rapidly extended and by 1890 the first deep-level route was built. This introduced electric engines which ran through circular tunnels constructed like tubes, which is why the name 'Tube' is often used instead of Underground. The first 'tube' was the City and South London Railway which ran from King William Street in the City to Stockwell.

The prophets of doom forecast that the end of the world would be hastened by the construction of these 'hell-holes'. They predicted that burrowing into the infernal regions was bound to disturb the devil, who would wreak devastation and cause disaster. The manifestations of diabolic forces and unquiet spirits were at this time seen as the spiritual phenomena we now call hauntings.

Despite this apocalyptic and dystopian picture, the London Underground has continued the tradition of pioneering new design for 150 years, giving London a legacy to be extremely proud of. But it has also had its dramas including murders, tragic accidents, terrorist bomb attacks and suicides. Hauntings are usually place-centred, and now the popular view is that they are triggered by drama and involve the ghosts of the dead. Add to this the numerous plague pits, graveyards and crypts that were disturbed during the building of the Underground and we have thousands of troubled souls none too pleased to have their eternal rest disturbed.

The unquiet spirit hypothesis remains a popular conjecture when dealing with visual apparitions, the sensation of a presence, anomalous noises, temperature variations, smells, object movements, doors opening and closing by themselves, and electrical anomalies. More recently other psychic suppositions have been offered as potential causes and it's been suggested that such hauntings arise from vibrations set up by tides and underground water, electromagnetic energy released from tectonic plates, man-made electromagnetic radiation and infrasound.

Whether the phenomena are caused by the devil, the dead or complex geophysical theories, the London Underground qualifies on so many counts that it's not surprising to find that it has more than its fair share of hauntings.

Ghost Stories of the London Underground is packed with these amazing stories, weird incidents and encounters that defy explanation, so come with us on a real-life ghost train experience through one of the most haunted underground systems in the world.

Jill Armitage

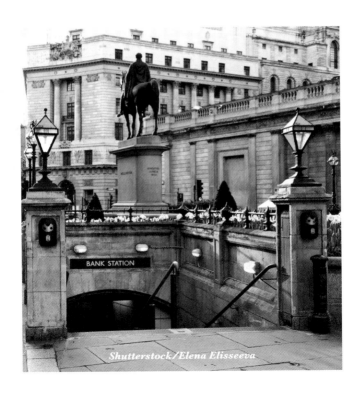

Shutterstock/Elena Elisseeva

HAUNTED STATIONS

When Railway Mania hit Great Britain in the mid 19th century, the race was on to build a rail network that covered the country served by railway stations that made impressive architectural statements. The Underground was different. Platforms and tracks were hidden neatly away below street level and this caused a problem when deciding where to position stations. Should they be at street level to create the same architectural statement or

A basic covering over a stairwell to the Underground

tucked away near the heart of the operation? In the latter case, all that was necessary at street level was a basic covering over a stairway down to the platform and track below.

The Metropolitan line's first three stations were wooden structures positioned underground, yet by December 1865 the terminus at Farringdon had an impressive surface building built in Suffolk stone with Roman arches and decorative roof finials. This Italianate style served as a model for future stations but many private operators opted for rudimentary wooden canopies over exposed platforms. To compete, surface stations became less fancy, and in the heart of London's expensive real estate districts the Central London Railway cleverly sold the 'air space' over their stations for commercial purposes. Over the years, stations have been rebuilt and refitted reflecting the style of the period so there is now no uniformity of design; each is as unique as the ghosts that haunt them.

Farringdon Station was the terminus of the first stretch of London underground which opened in January 1863 near the great Smithfield meat market. The station that now stands on the spot dates from 1923, and in keeping with London Underground's continual upgrading and improved accessibility, in 2011/12 it became the 66th underground station to be step-free from street to platform level – now shown on maps as a blue wheelchair on a white background.

Despite the upgrades and improvements, over the years there have been persistent tales of hauntings at Farringdon Station. The most reported is a young girl who haunts the station, and there are also screams that frequently echo down the platform as the last train leaves at night. These hauntings probably come from the time when Smithfield, or Smoothfield as it was originally known, was one of London's main places of execution.

Mary Tudor tried to undo the work of her father Henry VIII who created the Church of England, thereby alienating Roman Catholics and the Pope. As the daughter of Catherine of Aragon, Mary remained steadfast to the old religion and when

Heretics were burnt at the stake near Farringdon Station

she became Queen in 1553 she tried to return England to Catholicism, but her methods were very severe. During her short, five-year reign, she had over two hundred Protestants put to death for refusing to comply to her wishes. Many of these heretics were burnt at the stake at Smithfield. Burning destroyed every bit of the body, so it was believed that no dangerous fragments would remain to corrupt others.

For some of these victims their torment seems to be eternal. People who work in the area in the early hours have often been disturbed by agonising screams that rend the air, and the sickly smell of burning flesh.

Historical records talk of a no man's land established in 1348 in the Farringdon/Smithfield area where, according to a contemporary historian, some 50,000 plague victims were buried. Despite this, no one knows how many plague pits there are or where they are located, because plague pits were not recorded and were dug deep to prevent the spread of infection. Building the Underground has meant tunnelling, which has often disturbed graveyards and plague pits. In 2009, a mass burial plague site at East Smithfield was revealed, where the individuals were stacked five deep. Samples of DNA were used to analyse 100 skeletons that date from 1348 to 1350 and died in the Black Death.

This is one of the few areas of central London not developed, but now work in this area is proceeding on the Crossrail scheme,

Skeletons are regularly discovered while boring

an ongoing 14.8 billion pound project aimed to be completed in 2018, creating a railway across central London from east to west under the existing underground system. When a shaft was sunk on the edge of Charterhouse Square, Farringdon, on the site of a former monastery it revealed the remains of thirteen individuals lying in two rows, but could further excavations reveal those mass burial plague sites? It's believed that something from all the decomposed bodies has impregnated the soil and when the time is right, some form of miasma seeps through into the tunnels, thus creating a paranormal situation.

Liverpool Street is a busy underground station and a major station on the main rail network. Like all stations it is monitored by twenty-four-hour CCTV and any abnormality or disturbance is quickly investigated. In the early hours of a summer morning in 2000, when the station was closed to passengers, Steve Coats, a station supervisor with twenty years' experience, was sent to investigate the sighting of a man in white overalls seen walking along the platform near the eastbound tunnel. Steve went to the platform but found no one. He checked inside the tunnel to make sure no one was hiding but was quite satisfied that there was no one there. Using the telephone by the escalator, he reported back to the control monitor that there was no sign of the man, but the guy in the control room was totally mystified.

'He was there. You walked right past him,' he said.

'Are you sure it wasn't just a blip on the CCTV?' asked Steve, not sure what other explanation there could be.

The controller assured him it wasn't, so Steve went back, convinced that someone was playing a hoax. He still found no one, so again he reported back to the control room.

'How could you not see him?' asked his colleague. 'I'm telling you; on my CCTV, that guy was standing right next to you.'

Could this ghostly figure have any connection with the building that previously occupied the site, the Bethlehem Royal Hospital, more famously known by its nicknamed of Bedlam? This former monastery was converted into a 'lunatic asylum', a secure hospital for people with mental illness, in 1547 and its name became synonymous with 'madhouse'.

Bedlam hospital was meant to be a place of safety for dangerous or vulnerable people, but soon became a popular tourist attraction. As late as the 1820s it was possible to visit, and, for a fee, watch the inmates behaving in a bizarre manner. We'd now consider this very inhumane and degrading, but has the freak

Bedlam mental hospital plaque

show left a disturbing legacy? The mysterious noises like screams that are often heard here at Liverpool Street are supposedly the voices of former inmates.

When Liverpool Street Station was being constructed, 300 un-coffined bodies were disturbed here dating from between 1500 and 1700. As many as eight bodies per cubic foot were crammed in here, which might suggest a plague pit. The fact that Liverpool Street Station is only a mile from Farringdon, and an area where contemporary historians believe some 50,000 plague victims were buried, might just confirm this.

The land now occupied by **Green Park** is reputed to have been the burial ground for the nearby St James's Hospital for Leprous Women, the site of which was commandeered by Henry VIII for the building of St James's Palace. It's said this is the reason Green Park has no flowers. People considered this just another bit of London folklore until in the 1960s when constructing the Victoria Line the contractors ran into trouble when the boring machine tore through the burial ground, unearthing the corpses and traumatising many brawny navvies. Could this disturbance account for the phantom grey lady that haunts Green Park Station?

In the late 1970s while waiting for the traction current to be turned off, a young track engineer felt a slap on his face and turned to see the grey figure of a woman vanishing along the platform. Another man present saw nothing, other than the victim flinch and swear.

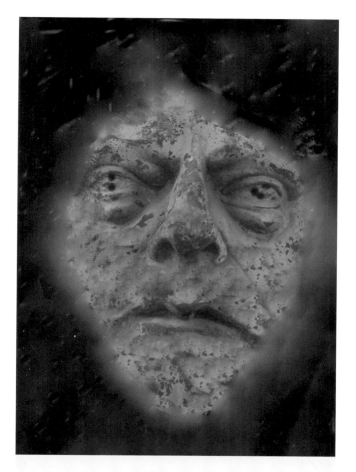

A leprous woman

At the **Elephant & Castle** underground station, Bakerloo Line platform, a young woman dressed in dark clothing is frequently seen by staff and commuters as she enters one of the carriages, walks towards the front of the train and then vanishes.

A member of the crew joined the train at the terminus at Elephant & Castle at around 6 o'clock one evening. He walked through to join the driver, but as he had not yet arrived, the crew member moved back towards the rear door as a young woman entered. She walked straight past the man, making him stand aside for her to pass. When the driver arrived both men moved to the front of the train, but the girl was not in the carriage. She couldn't have left the train without passing him and she was neither in the carriage nor on the platform. The only place she could have gone was into the tunnel, and that was a problem. There are fifty suicides every year on the London Underground and he was anxious not to make her one of them. The worried crew member informed the driver, whose response was just: 'Oh, her. We hear about her all the time. She's even been in the papers.'

Is this phantom also responsible for the footsteps that are heard running through Elephant & Castle Station when the platforms are deserted? The phantom runner is heard and never seen, but it has chilled the blood of many maintenance workers employed at the station during the night. In addition tapping sounds have been heard on the platform, and doors in the station have been known to suddenly slam for no apparent reason. Could this have

*A young woman wanders through the tunnels and boards the train
at the Elephant & Castle*

anything to do with the fact that behind the tunnel wall which leads to the London Depot lies one of the many London plague pits? Unless they have no alternative, few staff will go down there at night.

Harry is the Station Supervisor at **Becontree Station**. In 1992, he had returned to his office to do some paperwork when he heard the door handle rattle. His office opened onto the Eastern Line Platform and the door often rattled as a train approached. Harry waited for the train but, despite the handle rattling three times, no train arrived. He walked out of the door and onto the platform where he had a feeling of unease. Knowing a colleague was working upstairs, he made his way towards the stairs but felt as if someone was walking behind him. He turned sharply and came face to face with a woman with long blonde hair and wearing a white dress. Actually, Harry admits, 'We didn't come face to face, because the woman had no face. Every time I tell the story I get goose pimples just thinking about it.'

He ran upstairs and burst in on his colleague who took one look at him and said, 'You look as if you've seen a ghost.'

'I have,' said Harry, not expecting to be believed, but much to his surprise his colleague could describe the woman accurately as he too had seen her. In 1958, ten people died in a train collision on this part of the District Line. Both trains had left Becontree station just minutes before, so perhaps this young lady was one of the fatalities.

In the early hours of one morning in 1951, an electrician working on the platform of **Ickenham** station glanced up to see a middle-aged woman watching him. She raised her hand and waved to him, beckoning him to follow her as she walked down the platform. Thinking she needed assistance he left his work and followed her across the platform and down one of the staircases, but the moment her foot touched the bottom step, the woman vanished into thin air, leaving the nonplussed electrician to race off and report his strange encounter to the stationmaster. He soon discovered that far from this being an isolated incident, many station workers had reported similar sightings of the mysterious woman. It is believed that she is the ghost of a woman who fell from the platform onto the rails in the 1950s and was electrocuted. She invariably appears at the end of the platform close to where she fell to her death and waves to people as if to gain their attention, perhaps hoping they can stop the tragic accident that took her life.

At **West Brompton** underground station, a man dressed in dark, workman's clothing has been spotted early in the morning and late at night. He walks to the end of the platform then simply disappears.

A crash which took place on 4 December 1957 in the Lewisham area near **St John's Station** has left a ghostly legacy. Caused partly by fog, the crash killed ninety people and injured over one hundred more. On the anniversary of the crash if fog is in the air the agonising cries of these unfortunate victims can be heard.

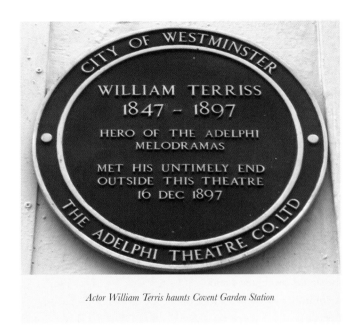

Actor William Terris haunts Covent Garden Station

One of the most infamous spectres seen on any busy underground station is at **Covent Garden**. On Christmas Eve 1955, ticket inspector Jack Hayden was writing up the log when the door to his office began to rattle violently. Thinking it was a late-night reveller lost in the cavernous depths of the station, Hayden called out, '*There's no way through here.*' But the rattling grew more violent so the irritated inspector leapt to his feet and threw open the door. He found himself face to face with a tall man in a grey suit, wearing a homburg hat. The man stared at Hayden without speaking, then he turned, walked towards the stairway and melted into thin air. Over the next few years Jack Hayden encountered the same apparition on no fewer than forty occasions, and he was not the only member of the station staff to see it. In early 1956 he was in the mess room with station worker Rose Ring, when a loud scream interrupted their break. Moments later, ticket collector Victor Locker burst into the room, shaking with terror and muttering hysterically. 'A man was standing there… it pressed down on my head… it vanished.' Others report phantom sighs and gasps, plus a rather unusual knocking in the lift. A tall, distinguished-looking man has been seen ascending the emergency stairs. When asked if he's lost or needing the cloakroom the man simply disappears like a bubble bursting.

Victor Locker's experience and his subsequent refusal to work at the station prompted London Underground to call in Eric Davey, a committed spiritualist. A séance was held in which Victor Locker suddenly cried out, 'Mr Davey, it's on you!' Davey later told the *Sunday Dispatch* he got the name 'Ter… something'. Somebody suggested the name Terris and pictures of the Victorian actor William Terris (whose actual name, however, was William Charles James Lewin) were brought and shown to both Hayden and Locker. The moment they saw him, they both cried, *'That's him!'* So why does a Victorian actor haunt Covent Garden Station?

Covent Garden Station was used regularly by actors at the nearby Adelphi Theatre. At the back door of the Adelphi

Theatre in Maiden Lane on 16 December 1897, an actor named William Terris was murdered by a bit-part player named Richard Price. As Terris lay dying in the arms of his leading lady he is said to have uttered his barely audible last words: 'I will be back.' And apparently he is.

One of the last reported sightings was in 1972 by lift operator Christopher Clifford. He had just closed up for the night when he was approached by a tall man wearing a waistcoat and hat. He remembered the clothes because they were rather dated.
'I'm sorry I've locked you in,' Christopher said to the man, and turned round to get his keys. When he turned back the man had disappeared. Thinking he'd gone down to the platforms, Christopher went in search of him but he'd simply vanished. Later, when shown a photograph of the actor, he confirmed that was the man he'd seen.

The story featured in a 2005 Channel 5 documentary when it was said the ghost has been seen many times. A 2008 documentary *Ghosts on the Underground* produced by The History Channel mentions another recent sighting of Terris at the Covent Garden Underground Station.

Wartime fatalities have left a ghostly legacy
(Paul Day sculpture at St Pancras Station

Wartime fatalities have left a ghostly legacy. **Bethnal Green** was the scene of the worst civilian disaster of the Second World War. When the sirens went at 8.17pm on 3 March 1943, 1,500 people tried to take shelter in the Underground. It was raining, the entrance steps were wet and slippery, the staircase didn't have a central hand-rail and the only light was a shaded 25-watt bulb. In the confusion, three hundred people were crushed in the stairwell as they tried to enter. One hundred and seventy-five men, women and children lost their lives. One hundred and forty-six were women and children. Since then, there have been numerous reports of noises that sound remarkably like women and children screaming and crying.

After the last train had departed one spring night in 1981, John Graham, station foreman at Bethnal Green Station, was locking up for the night. He'd turned the lights off and returned to his office to do some paperwork when he heard something strange. He stopped what he was doing to listen and could clearly hear the low rumble of voices. The rumble grew louder and was punctuated by bangs as it became more pronounced. There were sounds of chaos and confusion. He could hear children crying, and women screaming in fright. As the commotion grew louder, he was deafened by a combination of noises, ear-splitting screams, cries of pain and shouts of panic. John found it all deeply distressing and tried unsuccessfully to cut out the sound but after 10 or 15 minutes, he couldn't stand it any longer and had to leave. It would seem that John had experienced a time slip back to that dreadful night in March 1943.

Vic Tandy, who has been a lecturer at Coventry University for twenty years, believes there could be a more scientific explanation. He wanted to discover if the sounds heard by John could have come from outside, so he set up his equipment in the ticket hall, which has three entrances. He tried to replicate the sound of screaming women and children's cries but his experiment was inconclusive.

In the office where John had been that night, Vic tried to work out if there could be another reason that had triggered the sounds and upset John. He maintains that infrasound, which has a frequency below that of audible sound and therefore can't be heard, is responsible for a lot of spirit activity. The low frequency at which it vibrates can cause anxiety and is capable of causing visual disturbance. He set up an infrasound experiment and reported a measurable amount of infrasound which made him feel rather breathless, but it was not enough to trigger unease and give events a paranormal feeling.

One of the worst wartime tragedies to happen on the tube was on 14 October 1940 at 8.02pm, when a 1,400-kilo bomb penetrated 32 feet underground and exploded just above the cross passage between the two platforms at **Balham Station**. Massive quantities of debris fell into the tunnel. Above ground

Balham Station took a direct hit

a No. 88 London double-decker bus, travelling in blackout conditions, plunged into the crater created by the bomb. The dramatic spectacle of the trapped bus was to become emblematic of the dangers of the Blitz and a series of pictures of it appeared in publications around the world. The water and gas mains, along with the sewerage pipes, had been broken; water poured down, flooding the tunnels below, and gas hampered rescue attempts. Sixty-eight people died and the rescue and recovery of bodies took until Christmas. The station reopened on 19 January, but the incident seems to have left a ghostly legacy.

In June 1994, a former British Rail employee at **Channelsea Depot, Stratford** reported seeing a tall man wearing a cape and top hat. She was startled by his outdated mode of clothing but frightened by his terrible grin and a mouth full of white teeth. Just as she was about to approach him the man vanished, leaving the witness trembling with shock. A few months later, in the same area, the same employee felt a strong tug at her bag that almost pulled her over. She turned, expecting to see a colleague, but no one was around. After that she resigned and never worked there again.

A witness spotted a woman in her twenties wearing jeans and a T-shirt in May 1998 at **King's Cross** underground station. The figure was kneeling at the side of the corridor with her arms outstretched and appeared to be distressed and crying. There was nothing to suggest that she wasn't human until someone walking in the opposite direction walked straight through her.

Footsteps are sometimes heard echoing along platform 1 of **Tulse Hill Station** late at night. They are believed to be the footsteps of a railway worker killed as he walked the tracks near the station.

Over the years, the most reported and inexplicable sounds on the Underground are the ghostly whistles. Is this a contented railman from days gone by, whistling as he attends to his otherworldly duties? The sceptics among us blame the wind whistling through the tunnels, which can produce abnormal sounds. Another explanation is the whirring sound from moving trains, yet the most favoured explanation seems to be the whirring and whistling of escalator motors. At any one time, there are 426 escalators and 164 lifts in operation throughout the network, and it's these motors that are routinely blamed for the eerie sounds. It's hard to image how difficult and inaccessible the Underground would be without escalators, or moving staircases as they were once known, and the link goes back one hundred years to 4 October 1911.

No one was sure that this novel form of moving staircase would catch on, and the Board of Trade had just two escalators installed on a month's trial at **Earl's Court Station**. Most people viewed them as mechanical terrors, so on the opening day a one-legged man named Bumper Harris rode up and down to show how safe they were. People may have been scared to try them, but according to Board of Trade accounts the list of accidents during that first week included nine torn dresses, one pinched finger and a lame passenger falling off his crutches. After a month the performance of the moving staircases was reviewed and considered a success and between 1911 and 1915 twenty-two moving staircases were installed in the London Underground system. Now there are four hundred and forty six, but it's very unlikely that they cause all the eerie whistles because the noises don't stop when the escalators are not functioning. The motors are silent in the early hours of the mornings while the Underground is cleaned and routinely checked, but this is the time when most of the ghostly whistling is reported. In fact it's the time when many weird things occur.

In November 1978, station supervisor Barry Oakley and his colleague were locking up for the night at **Hyde Park Corner Station**. Satisfied that all was safe and secure, they returned to the supervisor's office but at around 2.30am were alerted by a commotion in the concourse area. Going to check, they found the escalator was operating despite the fact that they'd earlier shut down the escalator and removed the contact breakers, equipment designed to stop the escalator from moving. With the breakers out, the escalator was not connected to the power supply. It would have been necessary to use a key to re-activate the escalator, but as there was only Barry and his colleague in the building and they hadn't done it, who had? Barry was not

The escalator moved although it was not connected to the power supply

only totally perplexed, he was feeling uneasy and very cold. The temperature had plummeted to such an extent he could actually see his breath as he exhaled. He turned to his colleague, shaking his head in exasperation, but his colleague was leaning against the wall, as white as a sheet. He seemed to be in some sort of trance and it took Barry several minutes to bring him round. His only words were: 'Did you see the face? He was staring at us.' The poor man was so upset he went home and never returned to work at the station.

Members of the public also relate spooky stories relating to the escalators. Several witnesses have reported feeling an invisible hand placed on theirs as they come up the escalator from platform to street level at **Maida Vale Station**.

A spooky hand on the escalator

The most frequently heard story is the phantom stalker – although others have used a much stronger word to describe him. This mystery figure hangs around **Marble Arch Station** and has a penchant for standing up close behind women passengers as they travel up the escalator. One woman who experienced this turned abruptly and was able to describe the freaky phantom as dressed all in black and wearing a trilby. A second later he'd vanished.

Bank Underground Station, which opened in 1900, sits at the historic hub of the City of London and is named after that venerable institution, the Bank of England. To build the lift shafts and station, the railway company excavated beneath St Mary Woolnoth Church, buying the crypt for what is now the Northern Line ticket hall. The bones of the dead were moved to the City of London Cemetery at Ilford for burial, and the entrance to the crypt is now the seventh entrance into Bank Underground Station. Rather unsurprisingly this seems to have left a ghostly legacy. Maintenance workers have often experienced supernatural activity here in the early hours of the morning. They report being overcome by a foul stench, like the smell of an open grave, as one employee described it. In its wake there's always a dreadful feeling of foreboding and melancholy.

When the deep tube lines opened, access to the platforms was provided by lifts. Each lift was manned and at some stations in the early part of last century tickets were collected on entering the lift.

In 'A Romance of the Piccadilly Line', a short story written in 1919 by T.G Jackson and considered to be the first ghost story written about the London Underground, the ghost of a man who was pushed under an oncoming train enters the lift and the assistant asks him for his ticket.

The story reads:

As he made his way to the lift, he had an uncomfortable feeling that he was being followed. To be sure, a crowd was going with him but it was not that; he saw no-one especially noticing him, and could not account for the feeling. He had given up his ticket and entered the lift when the attendant said 'Ticket please,' to someone behind him. He turned but saw no-one.

'Old gentleman with you, sir?' asked the attendant. 'Why, what has become of him?' he continued, looking about him.

'No, there was no-one with me,' said George, much surprised.

'Well, I'm dashed,' said the attendant, staring about. 'He's gone anyhow. That's rummy;' and then he attended to his duty and started the lift.

I was told about a lady and her daughter who entered a lift at one of the main stations and pressed the appropriate button. As the doors glided together she saw a figure reflected in the satin surface of the walls, yet she and her daughter were alone in the lift – or so she thought. I was asked not to name the place so as not to alarm other lift users, but I can assure you I've never used a lift since.

Andy, who has worked for London Transport for thirty-five years, was locking up one night and making sure everything was secure at Bank Station. He checked the three lifts to make sure they were empty, but was only six feet away from lift one when he heard three knocks. He turned but saw nothing, so decided to ignore it. Then the three knocks were repeated and he was sure they had come from lift one. He went back to check the lift but could find no reason for the bangs. He walked across the ticket hall to the controls that turned on the lifts and flicked the switch, but no sooner had he done so than the doors of lift one burst open. These were old lifts with heavy doors that could not be opened manually, and knowing he was there alone, Andy didn't even look back. He just turned and ran.

Could this have any connection with events which took place on 11 January 1941 during the Blitz, when Bank Underground Station took a direct hit from a German bomb? The resultant crater measured 120 feet long and 100 feet wide and put the station out of action for two months. Fifty-six people were killed and sixty-nine people injured, so do some of these come back in spirit?

Perhaps the most famous phantom of Bank Station is Sarah Whitehead, whose brother worked at the Bank of England until convicted of forgery in October 1811, an offence which carried the death sentence. Well-meaning friends and family tried to keep this from Sarah, who believed her brother had just disappeared, but a visit to the Bank of England revealed the truth. Sarah could not come to terms with the news and from then on she would regularly visit the bank, dressed in black, asking where her brother was. She acquired the name 'the Black Nun'. Between 1812 and 1837 she kept up her lonely vigil and after her death she was buried in the old churchyard which was later incorporated into the Bank Underground Station complex.

Disturbing her final resting place may have re-activated Sarah Whitehead's ghost as she still appears to be wandering around searching for her brother.

If you manage to avoid the spooks and smells, use the lifts and walk the passages unscathed, the final hazard at Bank Station appears to be to make sure you catch the correct train. 'Confidence Trick' by John Wyndham is a ghost story involving a commuter travelling west from Bank Underground Station. The route goes via St Paul's and Chancery Lane to Holborn, after which he realises he is one of only three people on a train ride to hell!

Bank Station is now coupled with **Monument Station**, which derives its name from the Monument to the Great Fire of London. Officially the stations are known as 'Bank Monument Complex', although the separate names remain in use at station entrances and on the platforms and tube map.

Servicing five underground lines, plus the Docklands Light Railway, Bank/Monument is one of the largest and most complex underground stations and is the seventh busiest on the network. Because of its size, it is linked by some of the longest pedestrian corridors and tunnels of any railway station on the system. They are all monitored by CCTV and early one morning around 2.00am, when the station was empty, the CCTV camera picked up an old lady wandering through the corridors. Thinking she had somehow got lost in the labyrinth of corridors and been accidentally locked in, Cliff Archibald set off to find her and escort her from the station. Knowing the layout well, it wasn't long before Cliff could see her in the distance and he called to attract her attention. She looked at him, but there was no relief or surprise, just a vacant stare before she turned and walked away. Cliff was the one to show surprise as he ran to catch her up, but rounding the corner of what is known as Dog-leg junction, he found she had disappeared. At this stage he never considered that he might be dealing with the ghost of Sarah Whitehead.

He reported back to the operation room who checked 100 CCTV cameras but couldn't find her. She had simply vanished. Cliff checked and both sets of gates were still locked and padlocked but the old lady was nowhere to be seen. Cliff said that prior to this incident, which took place about twenty-five years ago, he'd always been a sceptic but something happened that night that he can't explain. He's still trying to find an answer.

There are still reported sightings of the ghost of Sarah Whitehead. Amateur film footage taken at Bank Station in February 2007 reportedly shows a deathly white face, while another shows a semi-transparent figure dressed in black with black hair and vacuous eyes.

Highgate underground station is in the vicinity of the famous graveyard of that name in north London. It is a designated Grade I nature reserve with 170,000 people buried in around

*It's claimed that a steady procession of the deceased leave Highgate Cemetery
and head for Highgate Station to commute to where they
lived their normal lives*

53,000 graves. In its original form it opened in 1839 when the inner city graveyards attached to churches had long been unable to cope with the number of burials. This site has serious spectral activity that over the years has inspired many writers and, strange though it might appear, there is an idea that the deceased do not linger around their graves because they don't want to be reminded that they're dead. It's even been suggested that ghosts actually commute to where they lived their routine lives, so does a steady procession of the deceased head for Highgate station every morning to join the land of the living commuter?

One final common claim in relation to hauntings is the observation that they become milder and eventually fade away, suggesting that whatever energy sustains them gradually dissipates with time.

GHOST TRAINS AND PHANTOMS
ON THE TRACKS

A confined underground system made up of a labyrinth of tunnels, platforms, stairways, passages and sidings can create a fear-provoking quality, but just imagine how spooky and atmospheric it must be when the last passengers have left. Between 1.00 and 5.00am, the system is not in use and the current is switched off to allow an army of maintenance and cleaning staff to ensure the next day's services will be punctual, clean and safe. This is the time when every mile of London Underground track is checked on foot by patrolmen, who walk the dark tunnels on their own. One such patrolman is Phil, who walks the newly constructed Jubilee line between **Baker Street** and **St John's Wood**. One night recently, he sat down to rest and was alerted by a noise coming gradually closer. Shining his powerful torch, he looked into the darkness in the direction of the noise and saw footsteps sinking into the ballast between the sleepers, one after another, as if an unseen person was walking along. He stared in disbelief, and felt the hairs on the back of his neck prickling with fear as they walked past him. Then the footsteps stopped and Phil didn't know whether he was relieved or not as he had to walk in the same direction. When he reached the end of the tunnel the first person he encountered commented on how white he looked.

Phil blurted out his story and the ganger laughed. 'You're not the first person to see that. Five maintenance men have been killed on this stretch and at least one of them doesn't realise he's dead and still wanders through the tunnels.' Train crews frequently report seeing an indistinct figure on the line from **Baker Street** as it approaches Rickmansworth.

The Jubilee line extension between **Green Park** and **Stratford** in east London was constructed in the 1990s and opened just before Christmas 1999. The extension carved its way through the grounds of several old monasteries, forcing the relocation of 683 exhumed graves. Ever since, numerous sightings of phantom monks on this part of the network have been reported.

As part of his managerial training, Paul Fisher was sent to walk the line between the **Oval** and **Stockwell**. Halfway along, at a place called **South Island Place**, he encountered an old man with a Tilley lamp. Paul was surprised because, for safety reasons, he thought Tilley lamps were no longer in use. The two men exchanged a few words in passing and when Paul reached Stockwell station, he followed the normal procedure of informing them that he was now clear of the track. He then commented upon meeting the old guy, and confusion broke out. No one should have been there. No one was booked in to be on that stretch of track and no maintenance work was scheduled. A search party was immediately dispatched from the stations on either side Stockwell and the Oval, and after twenty minutes the search parties met halfway. The old man couldn't be found and the first trains were delayed because of this encounter, but railway staff take safety very seriously.

Phantom monk

However, it was later found that the old man has been seen dozens of times over the years and is believed to be the ghost of a worker killed on the spot in the 1950s while working on a compressor.

Checking the tunnels nightly is not a job for the faint hearted

Vauxhall is on the Victoria line, south of the river, a line which didn't open until March 1969, but in December 1968 it had the rather unusual experience of being featured in an edition of *The People*. The article was nothing to do with the pending opening; it was because the line had acquired the reputation of being haunted by a giant figure. Said to be seven feet tall, and wearing brown overalls and a cloth cap, he was seen regularly by diggers in the workings, yet no one could ascertain who he was or why he was there.

Aldgate station dates from 1876, when it was built immediately next to St Botolph's Church, which contained the site of one of the biggest 17th-century plague pits in London.

Aldgate is built on the site of one of the biggest 17th-century plague pits in London

In 1722, the English novelist Daniel Defoe wrote *A Journal of The Plague Year* describing how '*they dug the great pit in the churchyard of our parish of Aldgate … about forty feet in length, fifteen or sixteen feet broad … nearly twenty feet deep … putting in fifty or sixty bodies. Then they made larger holes burying all that the cart brought in a week. The plague raged in a dreadful manner and in just two weeks they had thrown in 1,114 bodies.*'

It's believed that when the time is right, some form of miasma from the decomposed bodies that have impregnated the soil seeps through into the tunnels. Could this be why Aldgate station has a spooky air about it? Over the years there have been persistent tales of hauntings and the sound of footsteps echoing across the sleepers late at night. Sometimes the footsteps are accompanied by whistling.

In the 1950s an electrician was carrying out essential maintenance on the rail tracks at Aldgate when a station manager happened to glance towards him and was surprised to see a grey-haired old lady stroking the man's head. Needless to say, no such person should have been present. Moments later, a mistake in the control room sent 2,000 volts surging down the track, and although the electrician was thrown backwards and knocked unconscious, he survived the surge of current through his body and had no lasting effects. When told about the vision of the grey-haired old lady seen only moments before by the station manager, the electrician was convinced that she was his guardian angel who that night had saved his life. By touching him she had put spiritual protection on him.

In the winter of 1974/5, a gang of maintenance engineers on the approach to **Moorgate Station** saw a figure in blue overalls approaching, but before reaching them he disappeared. They all instinctively felt this was a former line maintenance worker who had been killed on the spot, and his appearance was a premonition or portent of doom. They were right!

Only a few weeks later, on the morning of 28 February 1975, a southbound train entered the platform at about 40 mph – the average speed is 20.5 mph (33km/h). Without slowing down it crashed headlong into a concrete wall. Forty-three people died and seventy-four were seriously injured. It was the single worst accident in terms of fatalities on the Underground.

The verdict was accidental death, but why? The driver was an experienced, reliable and conscientious man who moments before the crash had been seen attending to his duties. After the maintenance workers reported that they had seen a figure in blue overalls on the line, others came forward with similar tales of a phantom figure on the approach to the station, so did the driver see the same thing and panic?

The tunnels are haunted by former workers
(Bronze by Paul Day at St Pancras Station)

The stretch of line between **Gipsy Hill** and **Crystal Palace** is very hilly and between the two stations the line runs through **Crystal Palace tunnel**, which is reputed to be haunted by a former track maintenance worker. Many years ago, he was run over and decapitated in the tunnel, and since then his headless spirit is said to wander around searching for his lost head.

Steam-hauled passenger trains ended on the Metropolitan line in 1961, but London Transport continued to use a small fleet of steam locomotives to operate maintenance engines and various other departments' trains on the sub-surface lines. These trains operated mainly at night and the unmistakeable smell and sound of steam locomotives at work in the witching hours began to create a new piece of London folklore, that ghostly steam trains were at large on the London Underground.

Since the 1970s there have been occasional reports of a ghostly steam train which manifests itself on the Northern Line between **East Finchley Station** and the nearby Wellington Sidings.

The cutting that exists above the current **Highgate High Level Station** used to be a steam train line that ran to Alexandra Palace before it was eventually closed. During the war there were plans to convert it to be used by London Underground but these were unfinished when the scheme was abandoned in the late 1940s. The rails have long been lifted but residents still hear the sound of trains passing through the cutting where the track was laid. Until the 1970s, when the neighbouring stations were closed, a rational explanation would be that the sound came from the neighbouring stations, but they closed in the 1970s so how do we account for the sounds heard since?

Leaving King's Cross on the northern line there's **Hadley Wood Station**, a semi-rural station in the cutting between Hadley Wood North and Hadley Wood South tunnels. The latter is believed to be haunted by a ghostly diesel engine that was cut up for scrap in 1980. The ghostly loco is the diesel-powered *Nimbus*, named after a racehorse. In railway language it's the D9020, later known as No. 55020. It has been spotted running along tracks at Barnet, north London and disappearing into Hadley Wood South railway tunnel.

A phantom train arrives at the station

In December 1928, a passenger alighting at **South Kensington Station** found himself alone on the westbound platform. Although officially that had been the last train of the night, no sooner had it disappeared into the tunnel than another train pulled into the station. There was something different about the train, an air of mystery. There were no passengers, just the driver dressed in a reefer jacket and peaked cap hanging from the side of the engine. No platform crew went to meet it, then an ear-piercing whistle broke through the night and the train vanished into the tunnel.

When sitting in a compartment on a tube train facing across the aisle, it's hard not to notice your own slightly distorted reflection looking back, but imagine what it would be like if you saw someone else instead!

In the area of the **Elephant & Castle** and various other Bakerloo Lane stations, especially **Baker Street**, there have been many reports from passengers who were sitting and gazing into space only to look up and catch a glimpse of the reflection of another passenger sitting next to them, despite the seat being unoccupied. This usually happens on the northbound trains. This rather disconcerting experience of seeing a reflection in the tube window happens on other lines too but not with such regularity. The nearest rival is the Piccadilly line near **Earl's Court**. It's a scenario that is depicted in fiction in 'Non-Paying Passengers', a short story written in 1974 by R. Chetwynd-Hayes, in which the main character sees the face of his dead, despised wife reflected in a train window.

A murderer is reflected in the carriage window

A photograph taken by Mrs Woo of her nephew on a train on the **Bakerloo Line** underground in 1985 is quite remarkable as it shows a totally alien, weird reflection in the window behind his head. The image is of a man in an electric chair with sparks coming from his hands. This is not the kind of photograph used in posters on the London Underground and the train was between stations where the walls are blank. It is a sure candidate for a paranormal photograph. Looking for an explanation, Mrs Woo and her nephew from Malaysia were clearly visiting the capital and doing the touristy things, and one of London's most popular tourist attractions is Madame Tussaud's famous waxworks exhibition. Life-size wax models of famous and infamous world figures, past and present, are displayed in themed areas, one of which is the Chamber of Horrors. In there is a wax work of Bruno Richard Hauptmann, executed for the kidnap and murder of the Lindbergh baby in 1936. His waxwork and the image in the photograph match perfectly, right down to the number of buttons on his shirt and the way the straps are placed. According to a representative of Madame Tussauds they had made no posters or flyers of the waxwork, so had the group previously visited the popular tourist venue and taken a photograph of the exhibit? Madame Tussauds is on Marylebone Road between the Baker Street and Regent's Park tube stations on the busy Bakerloo Line. Before taking the photograph on the Tube, had Mrs Woo forgotten to wind on the film? A double exposure would be the most obvious explanation, yet the image is set so positively in the frame of the window and does not impinge upon the child, so the reason for this remains intriguingly unknown.

All passengers disembark at **Kennington** and the carriages are checked just prior to trains turning in a loop before the return journey. However, as the train drivers sit waiting in the dark loop tunnel, they report a strange atmosphere, and hear the connecting carriage doors open and close as if someone is moving from the rear of the train towards the driving compartment. These are unexplained incidents because the train is cleared of all passengers before going into the loop and there is no entrance or exit for passengers. Two reports of incidents that happened four years apart were related by Larry, a guard, and Bob, a driver, who together had fifty years' experience on the London Tube. The two men had never met but their stories are remarkably similar. Larry said the train had been waiting in the loop for ten minutes when he heard the interconnecting doors slamming. The sound was getting closer and he stood up expecting to see the driver approaching but there was no sight of anyone there. I spoke to Colin, who used to be a driver, and without any prompting he told me of his own experience in the Kennington Loop. As he waited he was aware that the interconnecting doors were opening and closing in turn. All the drivers are aware of this strange phenomenon and say it's the wind, but, as Colin said, 'the wind doesn't open and close a door before moving on to the next one.'

Such stories have been reported from the 1980s onward and are believed to be connected to a passenger who tried to board a train and was dragged into the loop, where he died.

Vic Tandy of Coventry University has a simple explanation for a lot of spirit activity. He blames it on infrasound, which has a frequency below that of sound and therefore can't be heard. It can, however, cause oscillation, vibration and pressure waves which can trigger unease and give events a paranormal feeling. It's also capable of causing visual disturbance and is sometimes called the fright and flight activator. Vic took his microphone and technical equipment into parts of the Tube where people have experienced strange phenomenon, and one of these places was the Northern Line Kennington Loop. He reported a feeling of unease and a staggeringly high level of infrasound, probably caused by a combination of motors and machinery. In the area where the stationary trains wait, the instrument measured 90–95 decibels of infrasound. If that was audible sound it would be equivalent to the deafening sound of a disco. Although it could make your ears ring and cause discomfort it's not likely to make those heavy connecting carriage doors on the tube trains bang open and shut.

Similar experiences have been reported by drivers and crew when held up by signals on the section between **Holborn** and **Chancery Lane** on the Central Line. In the partial light shed by the carriage lights behind them, drivers become aware of a phantom figure in the cab with them. Their uninvited guest stares fixedly ahead through the cab's front window, but as soon as the signals change and the train moves off, the figure vanishes.

It is the normal procedure for staff to check that all passengers have left the trains before they go through to the depot for cleaning and maintenance. The electrical supply to any train in the depot is isolated and the handbrake is screwed down to prevent accidental movement, but the sound of trains moving is a regular occurrence. Staff at **Addiscombe Station** believe that this could have something to do with the mysterious phantom figure that is often seen in the depot. He appears to be supervising the shunting of the units into the right position for their early morning departure. Staff on night shift regularly report the sound of compartment doors being slammed, and believe that their depot ghost is a former railway employee re-enacting his former duties. He's probably one of the fatalities involved in an accident at the site but he always vanishes before anyone can get a good look at his face.

DISUSED STATIONS AND TUNNELS

London Underground has a labyrinth of spooky passages and stairways

London Underground has a labyrinth of spooky tunnels, stairways and passages that are open to the public, but there are also many that are not. At the last count there were forty disused or abandoned stations. It used to be possible to visit them but since December 2000, with health and safety rules becoming increasingly stringent and the British public becoming increasingly litigious, access to disused stations on the London Underground is no longer allowed.

During the Second World War, many underground stations were used as air-raid shelters (see the stories of Balham and Bethnal Green). Some stations, now disused, were converted into government offices. The Central Line was converted into a fighter aircraft factory that stretched for over two miles, with its own railway system. Its existence remained an official secret until the 1980s.

A station called **Down Street** on the Piccadilly Line was used for meetings of the Railway Executive Committee as well as the War Cabinet before the Cabinet War Rooms were built. Down Street lies between Green Park and Hyde Park Corner. It closed on 21 May 1932 and is now a disused station, but the surface building with its bull's blood-red faience tiling designed by Leslie Green is still visible at street level. More recently it was used for the banquet scene in the six-part television series *Neverwhere*, based on the book by Neil Gaiman, a surreal story of a sinister world known as 'London Below'. Set in modern-day London – which is London above – the series uses the Underground to reflect an uncongenial city that has been left behind.

The abandoned station at Down Street

Down Street Station was featured in Episode 6 of the 2012 TV series *The Tube*. A member of staff takes the film crew round the station and on hearing a noise after a train has passed through the station, the staff member mentions a reputed ghost which has been reported by London Underground staff in the past.

Part of the Piccadilly line **Holborn** to **Aldwych** branch was closed during the war and British Museum treasures, including the Elgin Marbles, were stored in the empty spaces. On 25

September 1933 the **British Museum** station on the Circle Line was closed and became an abandoned station. Soon rumours began to circulate that the station and a passage which linked it with the Egyptian room at the British Museum were haunted by the ghost of an Egyptian princess. Dressed in a loincloth and head-dress the figure would emerge at night, but London Underground always denied the existence of such a passage from the station to the Egyptian room. However, the story was so persistent that a newspaper offered a reward to anyone who would spend the night in the station – but no one did.

The story took a strange turn two years after the closure of the station with the release of the comedy/thriller *Bulldog Jack* in 1935. The station in the film was called Bloomsbury but was based on the ghost story of the Egyptian Mummy. It included a secret passage from the station to the Egyptian room at the British Museum. On the night the film was released, more sightings were reported along with strange moaning and marks on the walls of the closed station.

The City and South London Railway was the first deep-level tube line. It had two 10ft 2in (3.10m) diameter tunnels dug between **King William Street** (close to today's Monument Station), and Stockwell, and was built under the road to avoid the need to get permission to demolish property on the surface, which is why many of the tunnels beneath the city curve as they follow the medieval street plan. The line opened in 1890 with electric locos that hauled carriages with small opaque windows that were quickly nicknamed 'padded cells'.

King William Street Tunnel is one of the oldest and longest disused tunnels on the underground network, stretching from **Borough** station (Northern Line) to the north side of London Bridge. It closed in 1900, but to commemorate its 100-year centenary in 1990, London Transport commissioned photographs to be taken inside the tunnel to appear in a centenary publication. One of the photographs shows what appears to be a silhouetted figure over on the left of the tunnel, although no one else was there at the time. A medium was called to the location, and claimed that the photographer had captured an image of the ghost of a man who died while breaking up a fight amongst the navvies while the tunnel was in construction.

Aldwych station stands on the site of the former Royal Strand Theatre which was demolished in May 1905. A station called The Strand opened on 30 November 1907 on the Piccadilly line but ten years later the name was changed to Aldwych Station. For the next 87 years a shuttle service back and forth to Holborn underground station was run from here.

The last train carrying the general public departed from the station on the evening of 30 September 1994. Today the station is maintained as a museum piece and film set while the ticket hall is frequently rented out for private functions. It is the most used of the underground's disused stations and numerous films and TV programmes have been shot in its cavernous depths. It has been used as the location for many spooky films featuring the underground including *Death Line* in 1972; *Ghost Story* in 1974; *Creep* in 2004; and *Primeval* in 2007. The 1999 film *Tube Tales* follows a series of mysterious and funny encounters based on the true life experiences of London Underground passengers. One of the nine stories, 'Steal Away', follows two young people escaping from a robbery they have committed. Using **Holborn** and **Aldwych** stations as locations, they try to escape and find

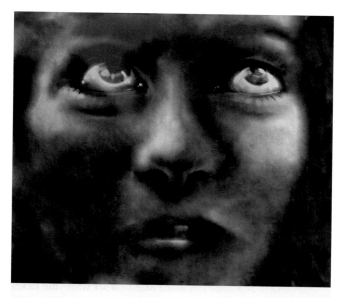

Prepare to be scared

themselves on what appears to be a disused station until a mysterious train pulls up and they board. Events soon take the form of a series of ghostly encounters.

The ground-breaking show *Most Haunted*, which has attracted a cult following in the millions, can choose from more than 10,000 locations in the UK which are officially registered and documented as sites of alleged hauntings, and twice as many that aren't. With such figures, they are never short of a haunted site, and one such place is the abandoned **Aldwych** Underground Station featured in September 2002.

Ian Pearse, Chief Engineer of London Underground, confirmed that they have had a number of paranormal experiences. There are cold spots and icy cold blasts of wind through the closed-down tunnels which feel very eerie at times. Barry Wilkinson, site manager of London Underground, commented on the tunnel's weird feel, particularly the quiet, emphasised by the dark. Most people have an irrational fear of the dark.

A fifteen-strong *Most Haunted* crew spent 24 hours filming here in 2002 and as Aldwych Station and the tunnels were used as shelters during World War II, to encourage the strong association with the war, the presenter Yvette Fielding and parapsychologist Jason Karl dressed in uniform. Both felt the cold, dark emptiness of the place, the silence broken by the scampering of rats. An estimated half a million mice and rats live in the underground system, and one of the scenes in *Tomb Raider 3* was filmed at Aldwych Station with Lara Croft killing rats.

Celebrity psychic Derek Acorah felt the presence of a male named Tom who walks up and down the platform. Derek described him as a tall, thin man who used to work at Aldwych Station, taking care of the rails. He had a seizure and died down there. He obtained the name Margaret, Estelle Bright or Brice but a search did not reveal any connection with that name and the station. She might be linked with the Strand Theatre that was sited here prior to the station being built. A woman believed to be a former actress has been sighted here many times and legend says that she was angry at the Strand Theatre being demolished. The ghostly actress is often seen strolling through the tunnels and walking along the platform where her dressing room used to be. The fluffers – those whose job it is to clean the underground tunnels and stations at night – have often encountered her melancholic shade and been terrified by it. The *Most Haunted* team witnessed a strange light moving towards them in stages, and the camera captured orbs in the tunnels.

A motion detector was set up on the platform where the actress is said to walk, and during the night, when no one was there, the alarm was activated. Stuart Torevell, the rigger who had set it up, said it was not a malfunction; something had definitely triggered it. The beam had been broken by more than just dust particles and it was set too high to be set off by a resident rodent.

If the *Guinness Book of Records* had a category for the highest turnover of cleaning and maintenance staff, Aldwych Station would be the obvious winner. Dozens refused to work there after being confronted by a ghostly figure which suddenly appears on the tracks from one of the approach tunnels. The *Most Haunted* team limit themselves to sites that have had recent sightings that can be verified by several witnesses. Aldwych certainly qualifies.

Embankment is a busy central London Station near Trafalgar Square, serving the Bakerloo, Circle, District and Northern Lines. Off here is a disused tunnel named **Pages Walk** which goes under the River Thames. After working there for three months, a contractor who wants to remain nameless had had enough of its unusual atmosphere. He felt there was something down there that didn't want him and repeatedly gave him signs that he shouldn't be there. Lights would go out for no obvious reason and doors would open and close in front of him.

Vic Tandy offered to do an infrasound investigation at Pages Walk and reported that the atmosphere in the tunnel was remarkably unusual. Being a sceptic, he was reluctant to say paranormal, yet he too experienced doors closing in front of him, but blamed it on the strong, almost gale force wind that rushes through the tunnel when trains are on neighbouring tracks. The direction the train is going influences which way the air is sucked. When half way along the tunnel he reported that the infrasound was of such a high level it might account for some but not all the strange happenings.

*Sir John Betjeman wrote a story about a nightmare scenario on the Tube
(statue of Sir John in the concourse at St Pancras Station)*

These dark, ominous places generate the kind of stories that create urban legends and haunting stories but how many are actually based on fact? 'South Kentish Town' is a work of fiction by Sir John Betjeman which certainly is. It's a nightmare scenario, experienced by a regular commuter who mistakenly gets off the tube at a disused station. The train moves off, leaving him in darkness. He gropes his way around and locates the emergency spiral staircase. He counts the steps to street level, all 294 steps, but as he nears the top, he bangs his head on the floorboards of one of the shops where the station concourse used to be. He calls but no one hears him, giving him no alternative but to grope his way in the darkness back down to the platform. It's a nightmare scenario – the feeling of being trapped, accentuated by darkness and fear of the unknown in the bowels of this labyrinthine network. What makes it more realistic is that there was a **South Kentish Town** Station on the Northern Line. It opened in 1907 and closed in 1924. The surface building with its blood-red faience tiling can still be seen at the junction of Castle Road and Kentish Town Road, and where the station concourse used to be is now used for commercial purposes.

South Kentish Town is an abandoned station that inspired a horror story

With its labyrinth of spooky passages and disused stations it's hard not to think about what lurks down there in the darkness of the London Underground. According to *Fortean Times* reporter Michael Goss, there's a species of subterranean troglodytic race made up of vagabonds, escaped prisoners, hybrid creatures and large mutant rodents that shelters in the Underground. Writers have been mirroring these ideas for 150 years so you can be sure they will continue to do so for the next 150 at least.

WHAT IS A HAUNTING?

Many people believe they have seen a ghost. The experience is as old as records of civilisation, but are there really such things? If so, they challenge all established views and ideas so it's understandable that we should look for some form of rational explanation. The vast majority of apparitional experiences take place at night, when it's believed that the combination of darkness, isolation and tiredness encourages the brain to enter into a relaxed state, making it more receptive to psychic impressions. The London Underground replicates the darkness. People are often tired and isolated. So is this the ideal scenario for experiencing hauntings?

Cynics tell us that there are no such things as haunting: they are hallucinations, a word that comes from a Greek term meaning 'to wander in the mind'. It's technically defined as a sensory perception that has no external cause and exists only in the psyche of the person experiencing it. Illness, drugs, exhaustion and sleep deprivation can produce a misperception, rather like a mirage seen by travellers who become lost and suffer from lack of food or water. Although feasible, this explanation becomes less satisfactory in situations where a number of people have had the same inexplicable, haunting experience.

Hallucination can be perceived by each of our senses individually or in combination: sight (visual hallucination), hearing (auditory hallucination), smell (olfactory hallucination), taste (gustatory hallucination) and touch (tactile hallucination). In addition, hallucinations can also affect the judgement of size (dimensional hallucination). So are the ghosts of the Underground really caused by hallucination? Judge for yourself.

Under the category of visual hallucination, numerous reports of apparitions have been collected since the end of the 19th century. Figures have been seen crossing or standing on the tracks, travellers encounter apparitions on lonely trains or platforms, train drivers report apparent collisions with figures, only to discover no physical presence on the track.

Descriptions vary. Sometimes the figure is said to be immediately recognisable as an apparition because of its unusual movement or attire. It may seem to float above the level of the track or be half submerged. It may appear in period dress. In other cases, people believe they have seen a living person and are only aware they are wrong when the spectral person suddenly disappears before their eyes.

After sightings, the most reported hauntings are those involving sounds. There are haunted stations and platforms where people have heard footsteps, creaking floorboards, doors opening and closing, and other sounds that have no obvious source. We could ask how these are created when ghosts have no weight to cause an impact or substance to open and close doors. On certain tube trains, there are carriages where the doors slam with no human intervention.

Passengers and staff have heard whispered conversations, whistling, humming, sighing, singing, sobbing, screeching and their names being called, only to discover no physical traces of any person or people in the immediate vicinity. How can these noisy phantoms make these sounds when they have no lungs, no vocal cords or any of the other physical organs essential to respiration and articulation?

The wind can rush through the countless tunnels, causing a rather eerie sound that makes the hair on the back of your neck prickle, but how do we account for the sounds from years gone by and from services that are long disused? There's the rattle of steam trains, whistles, whizzing wires and clanging of couplings all regularly reported on London Underground. These alleged auditory encounters are sounds that have no apparent external cause, but are they generated by the brain of the person even though they believe them to be external in origin?

Seeing and hearing a ghost can be scary, but possibly the scariest thing is feeling them. People have been touched, tapped, squeezed, pushed, pulled, punched, pinched, kissed and strangled. The sheer number of reported incidents alone makes us question whether these pushy poltergeists can really be dismissed as tactile hallucination.

We can be faced with the mysterious fact that we are able to detect astral aromas or smelly spirits that appear to be able to briefly assail our nostrils. It can be something pleasant or it may be a less agreeable stench. What these smells have in common is that in each case there appears to be no cause. Passengers may dismiss a sudden inexplicable whiff as something that's been drawn in through the vents, but train staff experience the smells of oil and sulphur that come from a previous age.

Until recently, people who experienced something that could not be explained by their five senses grasped at anything that might give the answer. Ignoring hallucination, they attributed such experiences to coincidence, divine intervention, earth energy, spirit guides, astrology or celestial events like the influence of the sun, moon, planets and stars on human behaviour. From this grew the belief that, alongside our five senses, we have a sixth sense, a facility that is able to gain and transmit information which lies beyond the usual five senses. It's also described as ESP, which actually stands for extrasensory perception, a term which is used to explain the receiving and sending of information by psychic means.

Despite the fact that it contradicts the fundamental laws of physics and continues to baffle scientists, psychic ability (abbreviated to *psi*) has long been recognised as a gift possessed by psychics, yet it's something many of us possess unknowingly. We all rely upon our senses to interpret everyday happenings whether they are sounds, smells or sights, but sometimes they are templates out of which all manner of things can be moulded by the human mind, bending reality to fit human expectation, legend and suggestibility. Subconscious suggestion, expectancy and belief affect perception and we allow the imagination free rein to interpret the images, sounds, smells and feelings. But what if we can't blame an overactive imagination or some sort of mental mirage? What was it that you saw out of the corner of your eye? Did you see it or did you imagine it?

There is a growing belief that hauntings are action replays. It's like looking at a hologram, viewing the same scene but in a different time. There may be noise and people may be speaking, but it will be to others in their own time. It is extremely rare if they respond to anything the viewer does. The whole scene is an action replay, with people returning and doing what they did in life, leaving an impression of a long-ago event imprinted like a time recording.

At one time it was thought that only powerfully emotive events, high emotions, suffering, fear, stress, anger and pain caused action replays. It is known that a catalogue of highly charged events tied to the trauma just before death, particularly if it is sudden or violent, seems able to send out some kind of psychic distress flare that permanently alters the feeling or vibes of a place. In these situations, brain waves, which can be recorded on an electroencephalograph (EEG), become more active, and when they reach a particular pitch it's possible that they can be picked up and stored by certain substances. But how can energy signals from emotive events become recorded in the ether?

It was thought that the events had to be highly charged in order to register, but that is not always so. Action replays can be amazingly trivial, a look back at what someone once did. The events can be anything that has somehow become imprinted in the ether, but how that happens no one knows. It may relate to specific atmospheric or geological conditions. Certain rock formations containing particular minerals may be needed to record and hold them. It might be that a number of atmospheric conditions, levels of humidity or temperature all need to combine to produce recordings. We are dealing with the unknown.

It's also uncertain what exactly triggers the replay. Perhaps it's the recreation of the same atmospheric conditions, or perhaps a totally different set of conditions need to exist. Maybe percipients with one set of 'brain frequencies' can perceive what others can't. Possibly a replay only takes place when a suitably sensitive individual presses the 'play' button. Could that person be you?

Have a safe journey.

FORTY TUBE FACTS

- The world famous logo, the roundel, a red circle crossed by a horizontal blue bar, made its first appearance in 1908.

- The tube map designed by Harry Beck in 1931 was voted a UK design icon in 2006. He was reportedly paid 10 guineas (£10.50) for his efforts.

- Busking has been licensed on the tube since 2003. Two of the most famous buskers are Sting and Paul McCartney, who have both busked on the Underground in disguise.

- The recording warning passengers to 'Mind The Gap' dates back to 1968. The recording done by Peter Lodge is still in use but some lines use a Manchester voice artist. The voice on the Piccadilly line is Tim Bentinck, who plays David Archer in the long running radio soap *The Archers*.

- The average speed of a tube train is 20.5 mph (33 km/h).

- There are three tube stations on the Monopoly board – Liverpool Street, King's Cross and Marylebone.

- In Cockney rhyming slang, the tube is known as the Oxo Cube.

- The record for visiting all the stations on the London Underground network – known as the Tube Challenge – was set on 27 May 2011, at 16 hours, 29 minutes and 13 seconds.

- Trains don't operate between 1.00am and 05.00am.

- Fifty-nine of the two hundred and seventy underground stations are listed buildings.

- One of the first stories to feature a ghost on the underground was 'A Romance of the Piccadilly Tube' by Sir Thomas Graham Jackson (1835–1924) although it's a rather misleading title.

- Straightforward titles include such works as 'Non-Paying Passengers', 'Underground' and 'The Last Train'.

- The Underground, including many fictitious stations, has been featured in numerous novels, films and TV shows. It would be impossible to name them all but the best known include *Skyfall*, *Die Another Day*, *Tube Tales*, *V for Vendetta*, *Nowhere*, *Death Line*, *The Eighth Light*, *Quartermass and the Pit*, *Dr Who: The Web of Fear*, *Mysterious Planet*, *Life-force*, *Ultraworld*, *Primeval*, *The Director's Cut*, *Bad Company*, *An American Werewolf in London*, *Reign of Fire*, *Survivors – The Lights of London*, *28 Days Later*, *Code 46*, *The Creep* and *Confidence Trick*.

- A census carried out on 27 September 1940 found that 177,500 Londoners were sleeping rough on tube stations. *London Revenant*, written in 2006 by Conrad Williams, deals with the drop-outs who haunt the Underground including the pusher whose pleasure is to push people under trains.

- The fictional station at Walford East which features in the long-running soap opera *EastEnders* is supposed to be on the District Line.

- Filming on location on the Underground costs £500 per hour plus VAT if you have a crew of less than five.

- The London Underground Film Office received over 200 requests a month to film in 2000.

- The first baby to be born on the Underground was in 1924 when the mother was travelling on the Bakerloo Line at Elephant & Castle. There were claims that she was christened Thelma Ursula Beatrice Eleanor so that her initials would spell TUBE but her actual name was Marie Cordery, The most recent baby was a boy born in 2009.

- One of the most famous babies, and now the American chat show host Jerry Springer was born at Highgate Station during the Second World War when his mother was taking shelter in the station during an air raid.

- During the war, special supply trains provided seven tonnes of food and 2,400 gallons of tea and cocoa every night to people sleeping in the Tube.

- An estimated half a million mice and rats live in the underground system. One of the scenes in *Tomb Raider 3* was filmed at Aldwych with Lara Croft killing rats.

- With 249 miles (402 km) of track served by 270 stations, London Underground has a staff of 19,000 and serves the transport needs of over 1,107 million people every year.

- A record number of passengers were carried during 2011–12 with 1,171 billion journeys made.

- In September 1905, the coffin of Dr Thomas Barnardo was carried in a funeral cortège on an underground train between Liverpool Street and Barkingside, east London, one of only two occasions this is known to have happened. He is buried in front of Cairns House, Barkingside, now the HQ of the children's charity he founded which has helped almost 60,000 children.

- The first tunnels were built just below the surface; later circular tunnels or tubes (thus the alternative name given to the Underground) were dug through the London clay.

- When the Central London Railway was opened in 1900, it was known as the two-penny tube as it had one flat fare. The 2d fare lasted until the end of June 1907 when a threepenny fare was introduced for longer journeys.

- The Victoria Line opened in 1968–71.

- The Jubilee line was opened in 1979 and extended into the Docklands in 1999; it was originally to have been called the Fleet Line but was renamed in honour of the Queen's Silver Jubilee in 1977.

- London Underground has four hundred and twenty-six escalators. Every week, they travel the equivalent distance of going twice round the world.

- The longest escalator, which is 60 metres (197 feet) with a vertical rise of 27.5 metres (90feet) is at Angel; the shortest is at Stratford with a vertical rise of 4.1 metres (13 feet).

- With twenty-three escalators, Waterloo Station has the most, but it's also the busiest station with 82 million passengers every year. During the three-hour morning peak travel time, 57,000 people regularly use the station.

- The normal escalators are the linear models, but a spiral version, a small section of which is in the Acton Depot, was installed at Holloway Road Station.

- Early escalators were made of wood but were later replaced with metal. The only station to still have wooden escalators is Greenford on the Central Line.

- According to a 2002 study, air quality on the underground was seventy-three times worse than at street level, with twenty minutes on the Northern Line being the equivalent of smoking a cigarette.

- In the 1980's at Queensbury station on the Northern Line, the figure of Sir Winston Churchill was allegedly seen on the platform waiting for a train. He once lived close to the station.

- A train nicknamed the Dead Body Train used to run during the early part of last century between Whitechapel through a now bricked-up tunnel to the Royal London Hospital. It was used solely for carrying the dead.

- On average, fifty passengers a year kill themselves on the Underground.

- In 1926 the number of passengers throwing themselves in front of trains was so high that suicide pits were installed under the tracks.

- The term underground is a bit of a misnomer because despite the growth of the elaborate network of underground railways in the city centre, only 45 per cent of the system actually runs underground. Because of this, between 2003 and 2006, the South London commuter services were rebranded the Overground network.

• London Transport Museum, Covent Garden Plaza, London WC2E 7BB (0207 379 6344, www.ltmuseum.co.uk) shows London transport from Victorian times to the present.

The London Transport Museum